Contents

Words printed in **bold** in the main text are explained in the glossary on page 44.

▲ *The* Karin B *carried 167 containers of poisonous waste.*

In 1988, a ship called the *Karin B* sailed the seas for two months. She was carrying poisonous **waste**. The ship sailed to ports in Germany, Spain and Britain, but nobody would let her unload the waste. It was too dangerous. Finally, the *Karin B* was forced to return the waste to Italy, where it had come from.

Recycling

Barbara James

Wayland

Our Green World

Acid Rain
Atmosphere
Deserts
Farming
Oceans
Polar Regions
Rainforests
Recycling
Wildlife

Cover: This huge pile of crushed cars, in the USA, will be recycled for scrap metal.

Book editor: Sue Hadden
Series editor: Philippa Smith
Series designer: Malcolm Walker

First published in 1991 by
Wayland (Publishers) Ltd
61 Western Road, Hove
East Sussex BN3 1JD, England

British Library Cataloguing in Publication Data
James, Barbara
    Recycling.—(Our green world)
    I. Title II. Series
    363.7

HARDBACK ISBN 0–7502–0135–5

PAPERBACK ISBN 0–7502–0589–X

Typeset by Kudos Editorial and Design Services, Sussex, England
Printed in Italy by G. Canale & C.S.p.A., Turin

Two American barges spent eighteen months at sea, looking for somewhere to dump their **cargoes** of stinking rubbish. These ships, and many more, carry the waste that nobody wants. Not all waste is so difficult to get rid of or so deadly, but what do we do with all the waste we make?

▼ *Greenpeace is a group of people who care about the Earth. Here, members are protesting about the dumping of waste in the North Sea.*

What is waste?

What happens to wild animals when they die? What happens to the leaves that fall in autumn? All dead plants and animals **decay** and rot away. Slowly, they are broken down by worms or maggots, **bacteria** and **fungi**.

All living things are made up of **chemicals**. When they die and decay, these chemicals return to the earth and are used again by living plants and animals.

How waste is recycled in a woodland

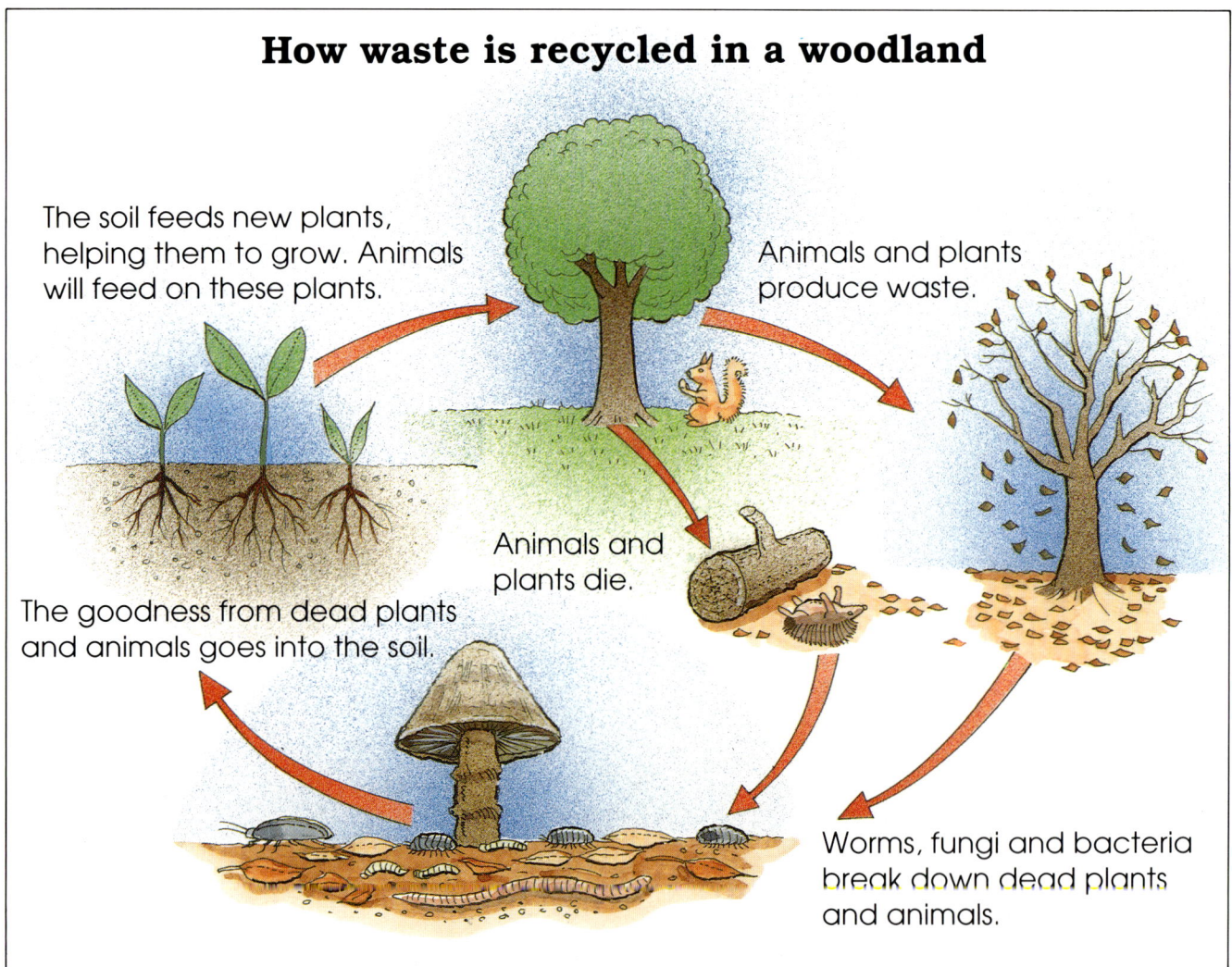

The soil feeds new plants, helping them to grow. Animals will feed on these plants.

Animals and plants produce waste.

Animals and plants die.

The goodness from dead plants and animals goes into the soil.

Worms, fungi and bacteria break down dead plants and animals.

▲ *A mountain of unwanted cars in the USA. Cars are usually recycled for scrap metal.*

▲ *A woodpecker's nest hole in a dead tree.*

Nature is very good at dealing with waste. But humans are good at making waste. Every day, 90 million bottles and jars, 46 million cans and 25,000 television sets are thrown away in the USA. Some of these materials are **recycled** but most of them are dumped as rubbish.

▲ *In northern Canada, polar bears sometimes look for food on rubbish tips.*

The Earth's recycling system can cope with some human waste. But people throw away so much waste that nature cannot break it all down easily.

Glass, tin and some plastics may take many years to break down. When materials like these are dumped, they harm the **environment** and cause **pollution**. Pollution is ugly and often dangerous – to people and to our planet.

Our wonderful home

The Earth is our home. It provides all the food, water and air that animals and plants need. It also provides energy, metals and medicines for humans to use. If we look after the Earth, we will look after ourselves too.

Household waste

We use lots of goods such as cars, televisions, **cosmetics**, books and furniture. These are made from materials called **resources**, such as metal, wood, coal and oil. Every day we throw away tins, sweet wrappers, food, paper, bottles and many other things. You may think these are all rubbish but they are valuable resources too.

◀ *Many of the goods that people use are labour-saving machines. How many can you see in your home?*

World population growth: 1750-2100

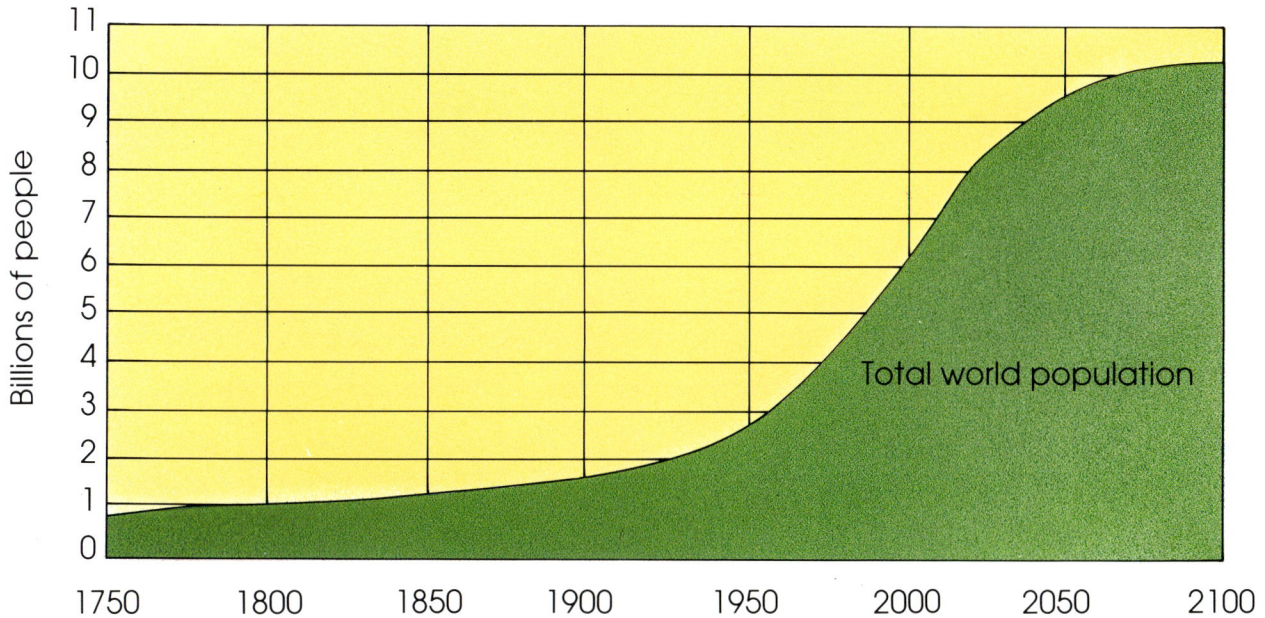

Billions of people

| | 1750 | 1800 | 1850 | 1900 | 1950 | 2000 | 2050 | 2100 |

Total world population

▲ *Each year there are more people in the world. This means more goods – and more rubbish.*

The USA, Australia and European countries use the most resources. Many countries in Africa and Asia are much poorer. They use fewer of the world's resources.

Who uses the world's resources?

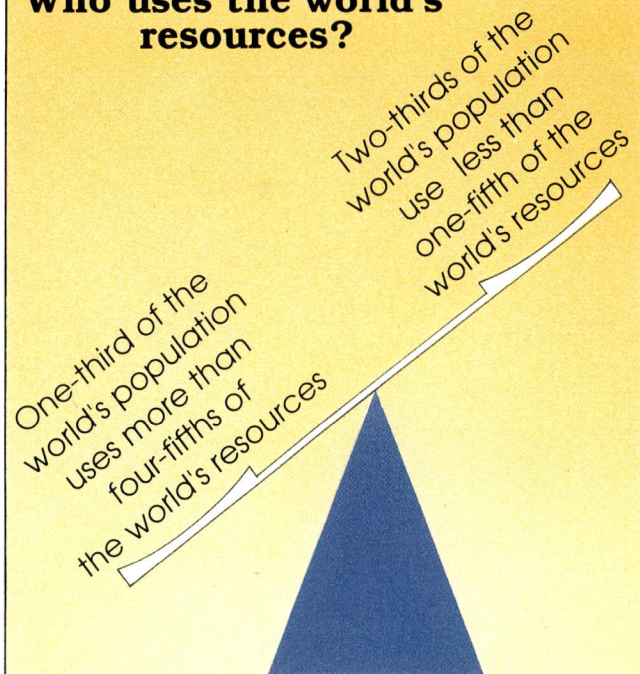

Two-thirds of the world's population use less than one-fifth of the world's resources

One-third of the world's population uses more than four-fifths of the world's resources

These people in the Philippines earn money by collecting rubbish. ▶

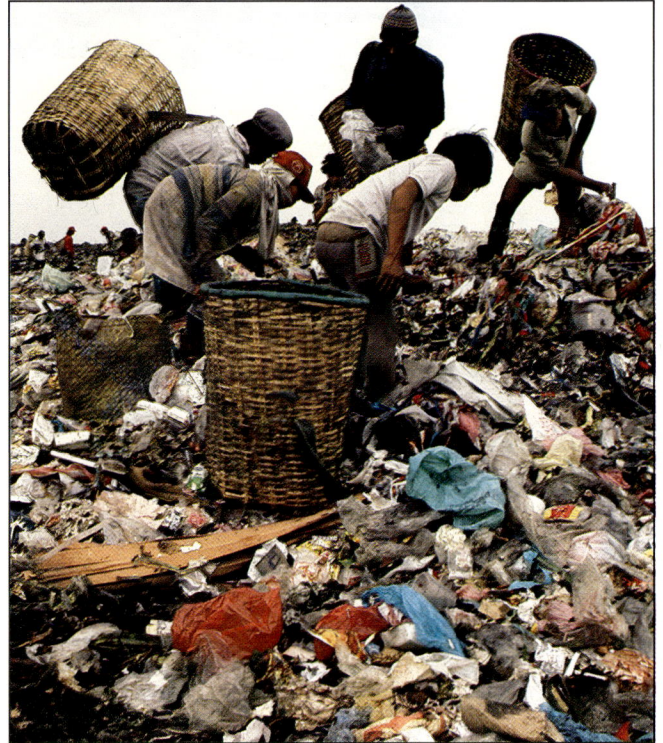

Every day millions of cardboard, paper and plastic containers are thrown away. This is called packaging. Some packaging is important because it keeps food products clean, but a lot is not needed.

The packaging in a box of chocolates

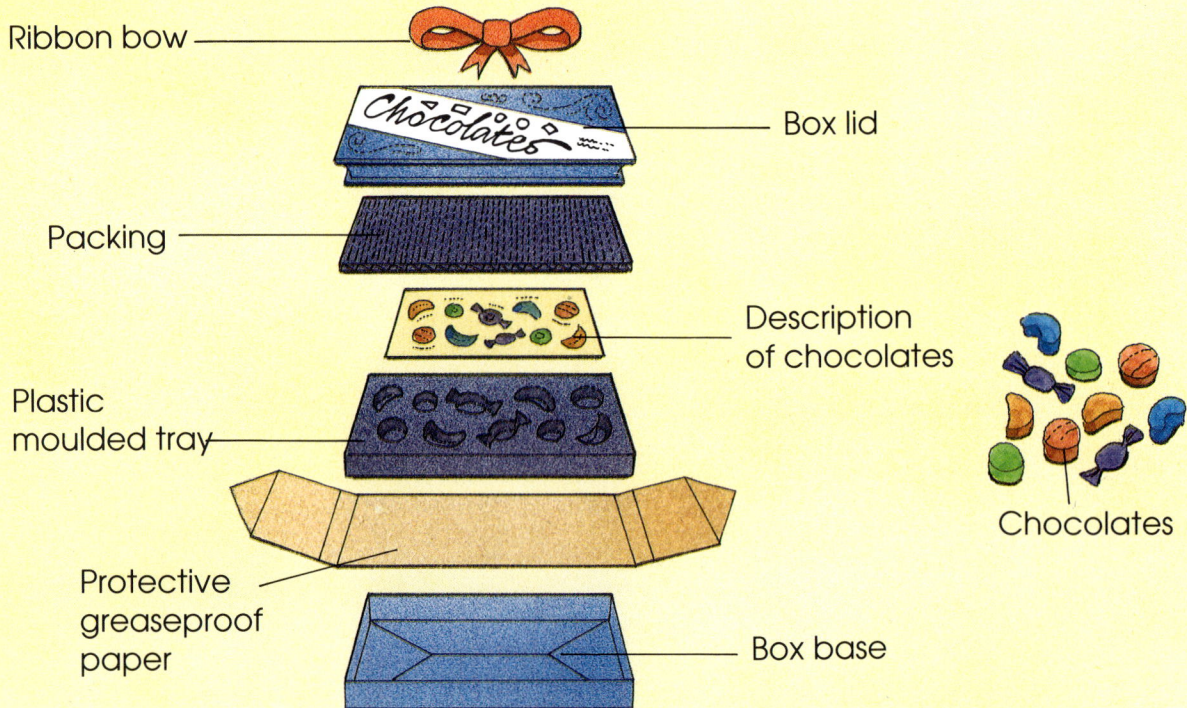

Ribbon bow

Box lid

Packing

Description of chocolates

Plastic moulded tray

Chocolates

Protective greaseproof paper

Box base

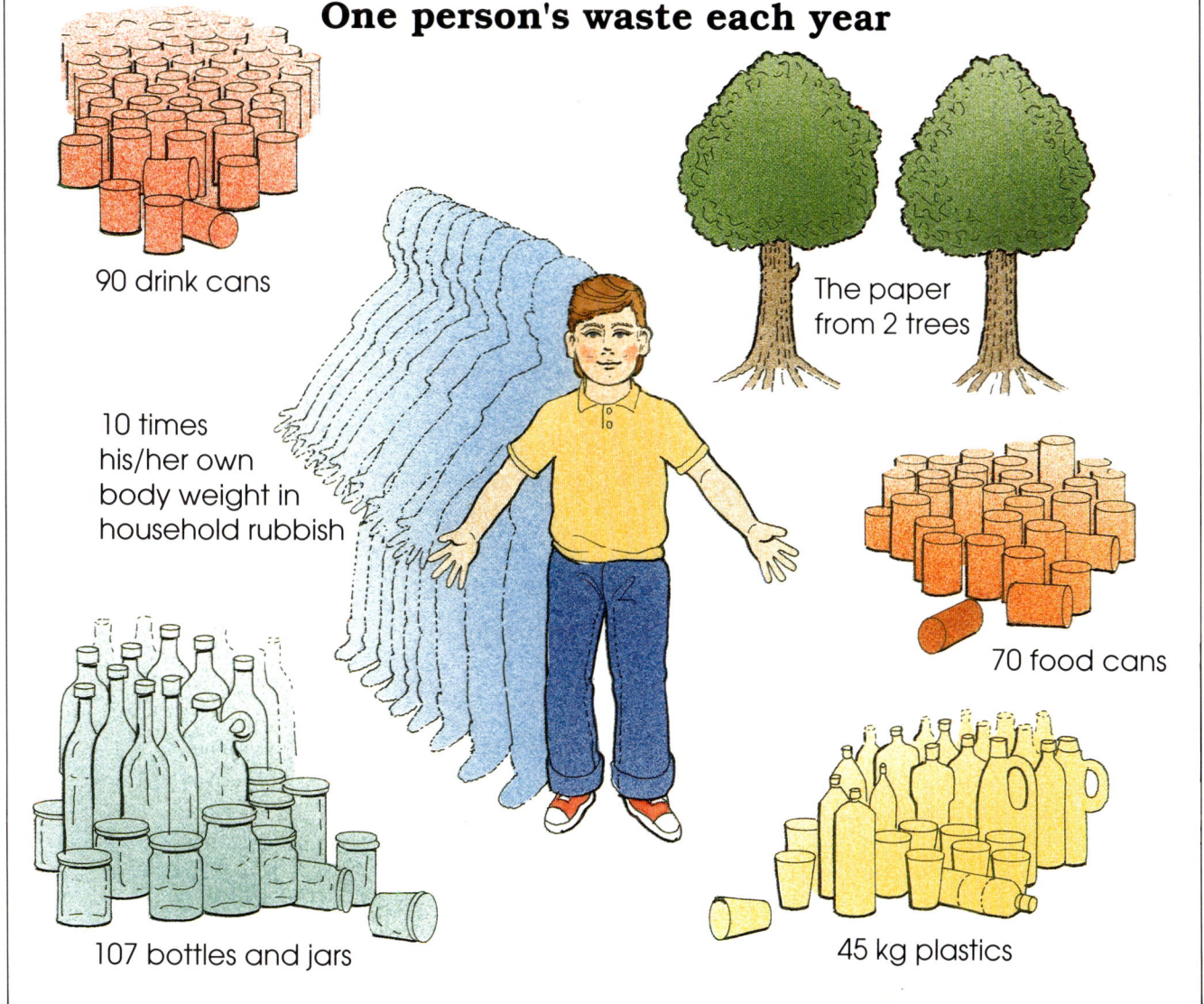

One person's waste each year

90 drink cans

10 times his/her own body weight in household rubbish

The paper from 2 trees

70 food cans

107 bottles and jars

45 kg plastics

Waste paper can be recycled and used again. More and more packages are being made from recycled paper. Over a quarter of Britain's paper is now recycled.

In Europe, most households fill two dustbins with waste each week. Imagine how much waste is produced by all the houses in one country.

▲ *Household waste is collected in dustcarts and taken to a rubbish tip.*

At rubbish tips, materials like scrap metal may be taken out. They will be melted down and re-used. The mountain of waste that is left is usually buried in huge holes in the ground. These are called called landfill sites. Sometimes the waste is burnt in a huge **furnace**.

Waste is expensive. It costs time, energy and space, as well as money. The state of California, in the USA, pays $1 billion a year to get rid of its waste. But rubbish does not need to be wasted. It can be **re-used** or recycled.

◀ *This picture shows waste being burnt. The energy produced can be used in factories, but the burning also pollutes the air.*

Glass, tin and paper can all be recycled and used again. In many areas there are bottle banks, tin banks or paper banks, where local people can take their rubbish to be recycled. Clothing, toys and books can be passed on to friends, relatives or charity shops.

◀ *You can help the environment by saving your glass bottles and taking them to be recycled.*

How does recycling help?

Recycling is a good idea because:
- It saves natural resources, like trees and **minerals**.
- It helps to solve the waste problem.
- It saves energy.
- It cuts down on air and water pollution.
- It saves money.

▲ *These waste collection centres sort glass, paper* ▼ *and metal for recycling.*

Industrial waste

To make all the goods that we use every day, we need industry. Industries **process** food, make chemicals, plastics, paper and many other things. To do all this, industries use resources such as iron, water, coal, oil and wood. But they also produce large amounts of waste.

▼ *Smoke from factories and power stations is a kind of industrial waste.*

Some industrial waste is harmless but some is dangerous. Dangerous waste is usually treated on the factory site first, to make it less harmful. Solid waste is often buried in the ground or burnt. Liquid waste is usually pumped into rivers or the sea.

But industrial waste often contains metals and chemicals that do not break down easily. When they are dumped into the environment, they can cause pollution.

▼   *This boat is dumping poisonous waste.*

Chemical accidents

Accidents can cause pollution disasters. In 1976, a chemical called dioxin leaked from a factory in Seveso, Italy. Farm crops and animals were poisoned. Many people had to leave their homes. Some people were very ill afterwards.

In 1984, more than 2,000 people died when poisonous fumes leaked from a factory in Bhopal, India. Thousands of people were injured and 200,000 people had to move away.

These men wear protective clothing to deal with poisonous waste. ▶

Waste from one country often travels through rivers, the sea or the air and ends up in another country. Traces of pollution have even been found in Antarctica, thousands of kilometres away from any industrial towns and cities.

◄ *Scientists checking for pollution in fields around Seveso, Italy.*

▼ *Some of the thousands who died in Bhopal, India, in 1984.*

Waste chemicals from factories are often dumped into rivers, which flow into the sea. Household waste, oil and **sewage** are all dumped directly into the oceans.

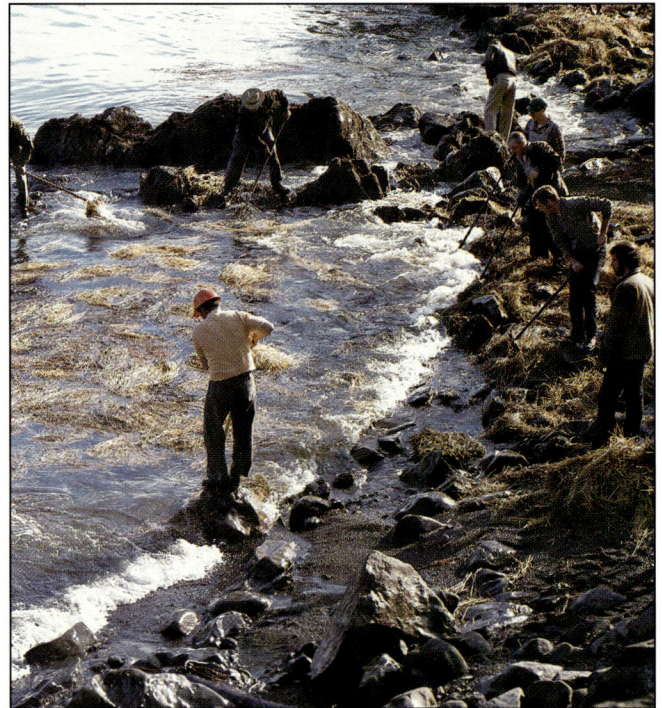

▲ *An oil spill has polluted this beach in the USA.*

◄ *In 1988, many grey seals died in the North Sea, probably from pollution.*

The beluga whale – poisoned by waste?

In 1900, about 5,000 beluga whales lived in the St Lawrence Seaway in Canada. Now there are only about 450. Scientists believe that poisonous waste from factories along the river is harming the whales.

▲ *This is a beluga whale.*

Many people think that the seas should not be used as a dustbin. Environmental action groups, such as Greenpeace, work to tell people what is happening and how to stop it.

▲ *Members of Greenpeace trying to stop a ship dumping waste in the Atlantic Ocean.*

War on waste

Waste Watch is a British organization that has declared war on waste. It helps people to cut down on their waste and set up recycling schemes. Waste Watch also talks to politicians (the people who run the country) and businessmen about saving waste.

In many countries, there are now laws to control the dumping of waste. And some countries are working together to protect the seas. But these changes take a long time to happen.

Farm waste

During the last thirty years farms have changed. Once, farm animals were kept in fields. Today many more animals are farmed and now they are kept in smaller areas, often indoors. Farmers can produce more food this way.

▼ *On this Australian farm, cattle are kept in small pens.*

▲ *If fertilizers are washed into rivers, tiny plants (algae) grow fast and soon cover the water, using up the oxygen.*

▲ *A slurry pit on a farm.*

This change in farming means more animals and more **dung**. Animal dung (called slurry) is stored in pits on the farm. Some of the slurry is spread on to the fields as a **fertilizer**. If there is too much, it can seep into the water in the ground or into rivers and streams. This can cause water pollution.

Farmers often add **artificial** fertilizers to their fields to make the soil better for plants. Sometimes rain washes these fertilizer chemicals from the soil into the **groundwater** or into rivers and streams. The waters can become polluted by the chemicals. Rivers and streams are used for our drinking water, so it is important to keep them clean.

▼ *This diagram shows how farm waste can enter rivers and the sea.*

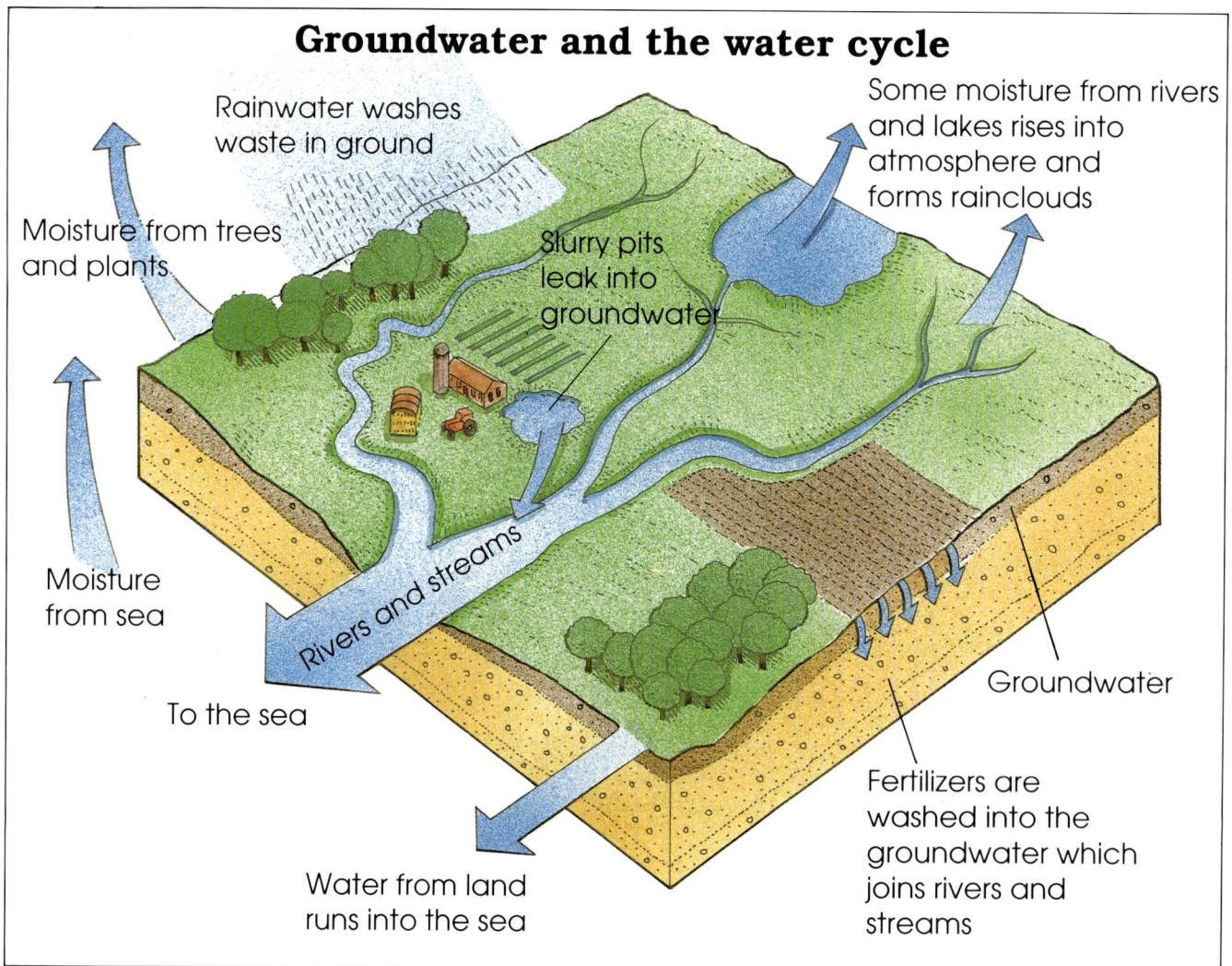

Groundwater and the water cycle

Rainwater washes waste in ground

Some moisture from rivers and lakes rises into atmosphere and forms rainclouds

Moisture from trees and plants

Slurry pits leak into groundwater

Moisture from sea

Rivers and streams

To the sea

Groundwater

Water from land runs into the sea

Fertilizers are washed into the groundwater which joins rivers and streams

Too much food?

In the **European Community** and the USA farmers produce too much food. To keep the food prices from falling, the extra food is destroyed or stored. Growing less food would mean less waste, but farmers earn their living by growing food. In the USA, the government buys some of the extra milk, grain and meat and gives some to schools for school lunches.

▲ *Lunchtime at a school in the USA.*

▲ *Farmers in the USA grow more wheat than is needed.*

Radioactive waste

In 1896 a French scientist, Antoine Becquerel, was studying a metal called uranium. By chance, he placed the uranium close to a photographic plate. When he looked at the plate some time later, he saw unusual dark marks upon it. The uranium was giving out particles (or 'rays') which had marked the photographic plate. This was the discovery of radiation.

When materials give off radiation, they are said to be radioactive.

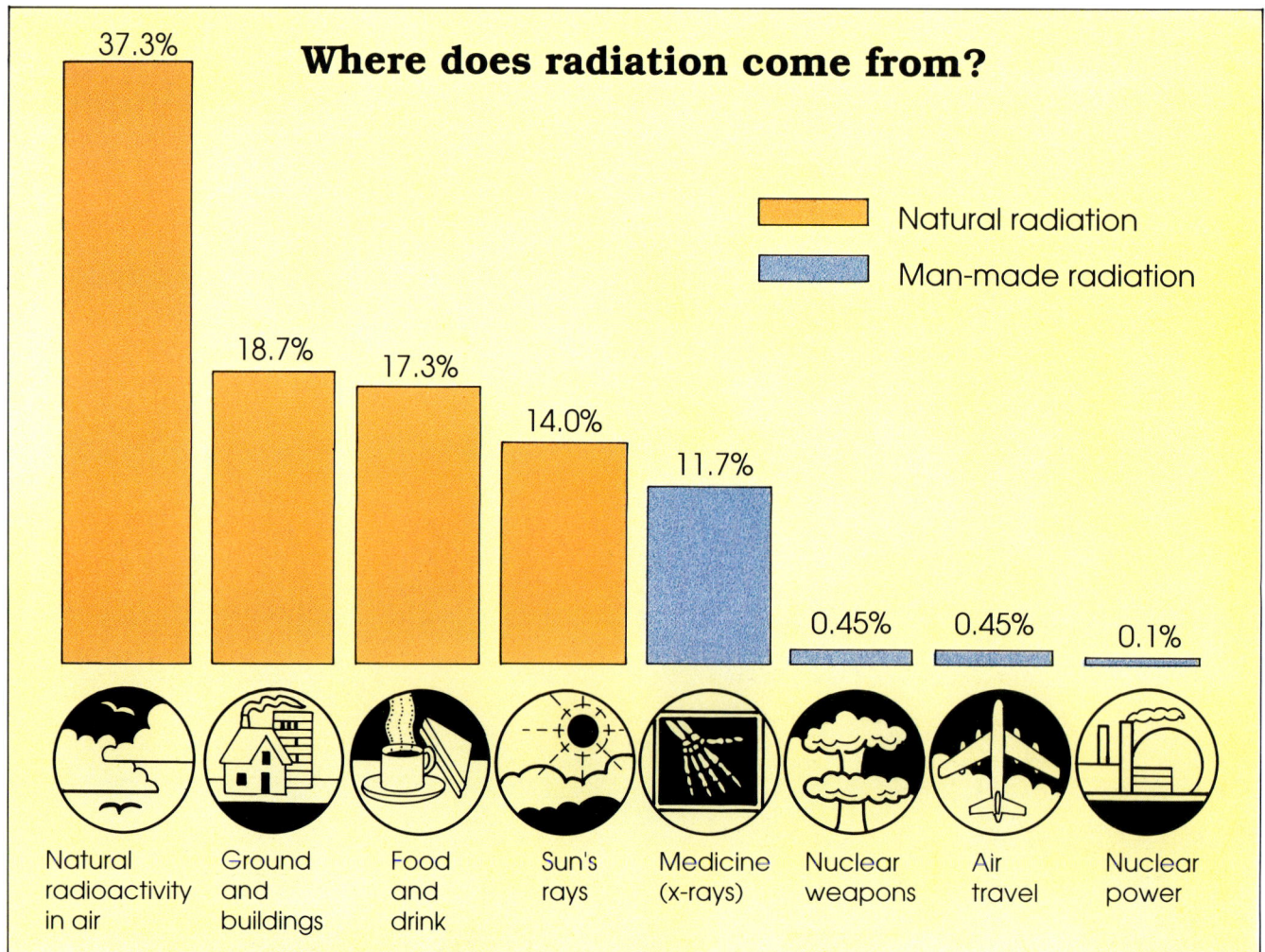

Where does radiation come from?

- Natural radiation
- Man-made radiation

Source	Percentage
Natural radioactivity in air	37.3%
Ground and buildings	18.7%
Food and drink	17.3%
Sun's rays	14.0%
Medicine (x-rays)	11.7%
Nuclear weapons	0.45%
Air travel	0.45%
Nuclear power	0.1%

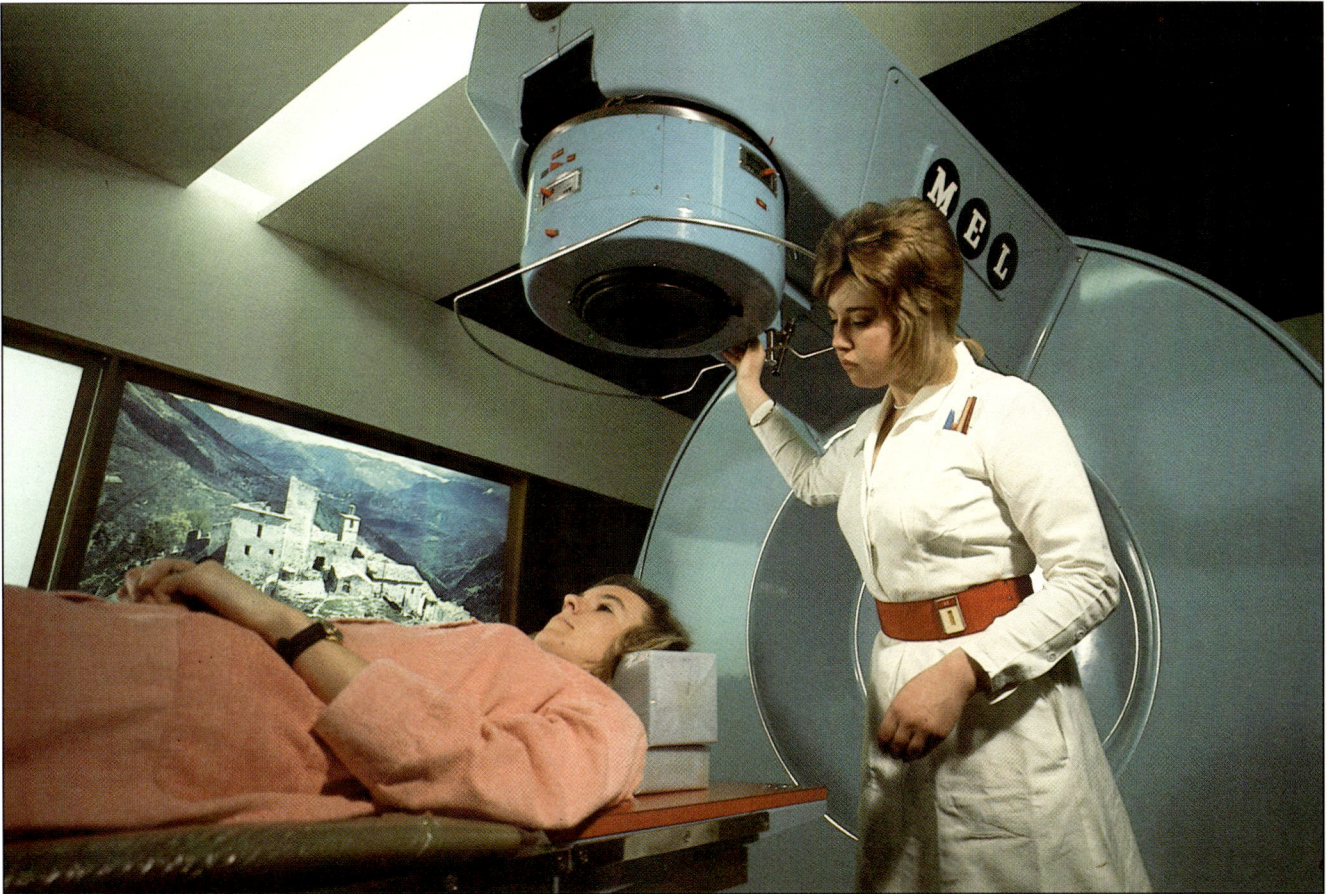

▲ *Radiation is used in hospitals to treat cancer.*

Radiation can be harmful to humans and other animals because it can damage living **cells**. The more radiation, the greater the chance of damage. Because radiation can kill cells, it has been used in hospitals to kill cancer cells in the human body.

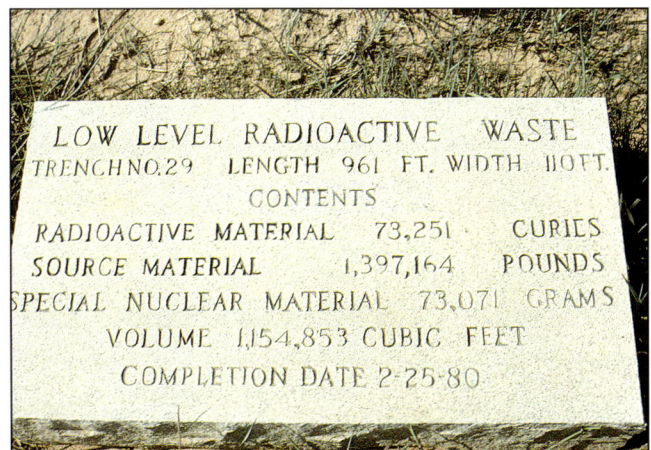

LOW LEVEL RADIOACTIVE WASTE
TRENCH NO. 29   LENGTH 961 FT. WIDTH 110 FT.
CONTENTS
RADIOACTIVE MATERIAL   73,251   CURIES
SOURCE MATERIAL   1,397,164   POUNDS
SPECIAL NUCLEAR MATERIAL 73,071 GRAMS
VOLUME 1,154,853 CUBIC FEET
COMPLETION DATE 2-25-80

▲ *This marker shows where radioactive waste is buried.*

Radioactive materials are used for **nuclear power** and nuclear weapons. They are also used in factories and hospitals. They all produce radioactive waste.

Some radioactive materials take millions of years to lose their radioactivity. This waste must be stored safely.

▼ *Radioactive waste being taken to a special waste site.*

▲ *These German members of Greenpeace are trying to stop a Swedish ship from bringing radioactive waste into Germany.*

Radioactivity cannot be seen, touched, smelt or tasted, but we can measure it using an instrument called a Geiger counter. Because it is invisible and can be so dangerous, some people are worried about how to get rid of radioactive waste.

Producing energy – the risks

We use lots of energy in our homes, for transport and to provide power for industry. Electricity is an important form of energy. It is produced at power stations using coal, oil or nuclear energy. After the electricity has been made, waste materials, gases and chemicals are left over. This waste can spoil the environment. Energy production can be dangerous. Sometimes serious accidents happen.

This oil rig explosion in the North Sea killed 167 people in 1988.

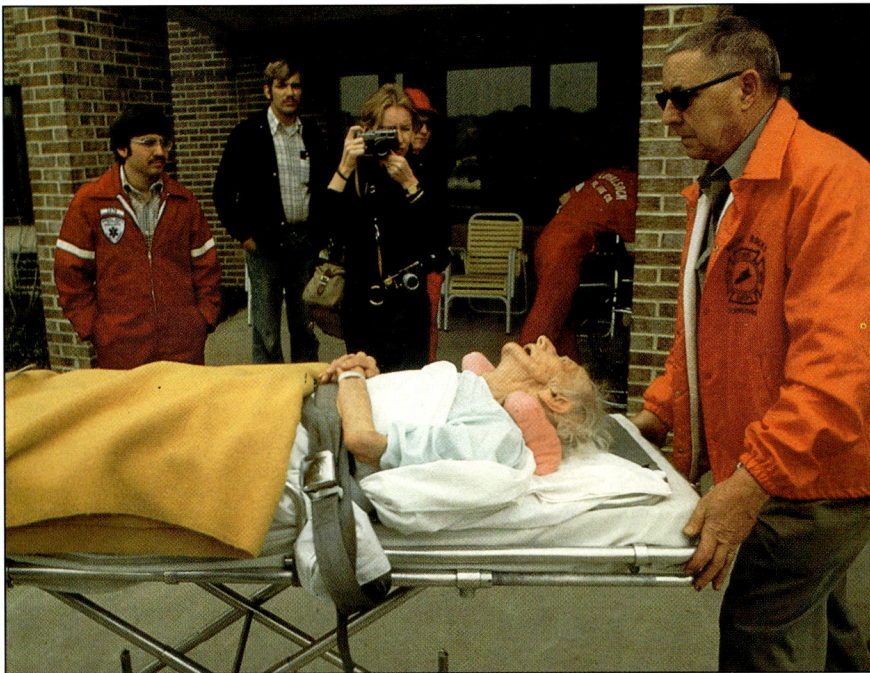

In 1979, a nuclear accident happened at Three Mile Island, USA. Many people had to leave their homes.

Nuclear accidents are very dangerous. At the Chernobyl nuclear power station, in the USSR, there was a huge explosion and fire in 1986. Local people had to leave their homes, and the area will be radioactive for many years to come. Some radioactive dust was carried by winds to other countries, such as Sweden and Britain.

▲ *Fruit being tested for radioactivity.*

What happens to the sewage we put down the sink and the toilet? In most areas it passes along large pipes called sewers to a sewage treatment works. Here, liquids are cleaned and put back into rivers. The solids are spread on farmland or dumped at sea.

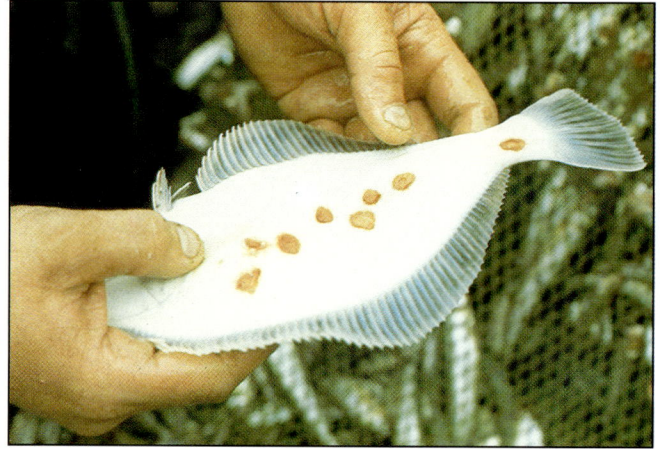

▲ *Fish can be poisoned by wastes dumped at sea.*

▼ *This beach in the USA is polluted with sewage.*

WARNING
SEWAGE DISCHARGE
DO NOT USE
BEACH OR WATER
S.F. DEPT. PUBLIC HEALTH

▲ *This American beach is empty because dangerous hospital waste has been washed up on it.*

Hospitals have to get rid of used bandages, **syringes** and waste medicines. These wastes may have been in contact with people who have serious diseases, so they must be disposed of safely. Medical waste is usually burnt at the hospital.

Gases from car exhaust pipes cause air pollution and can harm children and unborn babies. But now lead-free petrol is sold in many countries, and new cars are often fitted with **catalytic converters**. These make harmful exhaust gases safer.

▲ *Vehicle exhaust fumes are harmful.*

▼ *This car runs on methane gas produced by dung.*

This long Canadian bus can carry many passengers in one trip.

How can we cut down the pollution from vehicles?
We could travel by bus or train, or share a lift in one car.

Litter

Thrown away sweet papers, bus tickets, drink cans, bottles and plastic bags are all litter. It can be dangerous as well as ugly.

A rescued moorhen. It was found tangled up in an old fishing line. ▶

The European Community produces 17,000 million tonnes of waste each year.

People all over the world are beginning to understand that they need to look after 'Mother Earth'. We must stop wasting her resources, and polluting the land, seas and air.

◀ *These children are helping to clean up a polluted lake.*

▲ *These people belong to the German party called 'the Greens'. They believe in protecting the environment.*

Today many people are working to keep the Earth healthy in lots of different ways. People often join special 'green' or **conservation** groups. These groups work hard to stop pollution, and to protect wildlife and wild areas. They also try to make cities better places in which to live. Groups like this help people to find out what is happening to our world.

▲ *These people protested against plans to dump radioactive waste in Essex, Britain. They managed to stop the dumping.*

We can all make changes to help our world. Many people join 'green' groups. Some people change their way of life. They may decide to recycle all their waste, or to travel by bus or bicycle when they can. Many countries now have laws to help stop pollution. They also encourage people to recycle waste, save energy and look after wildlife.

Everyone can do something to reduce waste and help the environment. Turn to page 42 to see how you can help.

▼ *The European Community is working to clean up beaches. But many beaches are still very dirty.*

Keeping a eye on the world

The United Nations is an organization that brings all the countries of the world together to try to solve world problems. It has an Environment Programme which checks the health of the world. It keeps computer records on dangerous chemicals, and suggests the best ways to transport and get rid of poisonous wastes.

What you can do

Every day, New York has to get rid of 24,000 tonnes of waste.

Many towns have places to leave waste paper for recycling. ▶

It's your world that needs help, so what can you do?

Some useful tips

- Use both sides of paper when you write or draw.
- Use recycled paper when you can.
- Do not buy goods with too much packaging.
- Don't accept an extra paper or plastic bag in shops.
- Don't take more food than you can eat!
- Save energy – switch off lights and heaters in rooms not being used; wear an extra sweater rather than turn up the heating.
- Don't drop litter – put it in a litter bin.
- Give your old clothes, old toys, books and games to a charity shop.
- Many towns have places to leave waste paper for recycling. Take your waste paper to the collection point.
- Take used cans to a can bank (but wash and squash them first).
- Take used glass to a bottle bank.
- Return waste medicines to a chemist, so that they can be disposed of safely.

You can learn more about the environment from books, or by writing to some of the addresses listed on page 46. They will send information and details of how you can help.

If we keep our planet healthy, our lives will be better too.

A seabird being cleaned. *It was covered in oil* *dumped at sea.* ▶

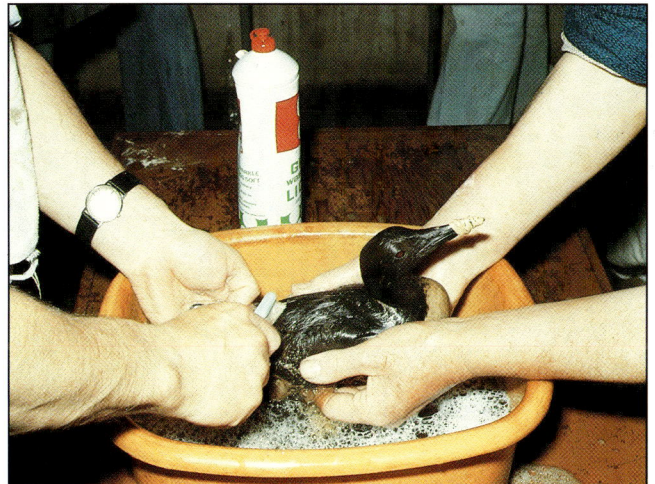

The Bellarmine Beasties

In Pollock, Scotland, a group of schoolchildren belong to a club called the Bellarmine Beasties. They decided their school was too dirty. So they picked up litter from the playground and cleaned up a local pond. Often they cleaned up at lunchtime or after school. Now their school area is much nicer. Could you do the same in your area?

Glossary

Artificial Used to describe something made by people, and not found naturally.

Bacteria Microscopic (very tiny) creatures. They are important in helping things decay.

Cargoes Goods carried by a ship.

Catalytic converter A filter fitted to car exhausts to help remove pollution.

Cells The smallest units of an animal or plant.

Chemicals Substances which can cause changes to living things in the environment.

Conservation Looking after the environment and using natural resources carefully. Conservation groups are people who work together to try and protect the environment.

Cosmetics Make-up, such as lipstick and eye shadow.

Decay Decompose. Break down and rot, and in doing so return goodness to the soil.

Dung Animal droppings.

Environment The surroundings of humans and all other animals and plants. Surroundings include air, water, soil and other plants and animals.

European Community (EC) A group of European countries which work together.

Fertilizer A substance which is used to help plants grow. It can be natural or made by humans (artificial).

Fungi Plants such as toadstools, mushrooms and mould.

Furnace A fire enclosed in a fire-proof casing which reaches a very high temperature.

Groundwater Water held in underground rocks and soil.

Minerals Substances, such as coal and tin, formed naturally in rocks and soil.

Nuclear power Electricity produced using radioactive materials.

Pollution Harmful substances, such as litter, factory smoke, and poisonous wastes, that damage the environment.

Process To treat in a special way. For example, in the food industry, to make raw fish into fishfingers.

Recycle To process waste products so they can be used again.

Resource Anything which is useful to living animals and plants. For example, oil is a very useful resource to humans.

Re-use To use something again, rather than throw it away.

Sewage The waste products and water that we flush down the sink, drain or toilet.

Syringes Special needles used to inject medicines into people.

Waste Something left over or not used.

Finding out more

Useful addresses

Council for Environmental
  Education
University of Reading
London Road
Reading RG1 5AQ

Friends of the Earth (UK)
26-28 Underwood Street
London N1 7JQ

Greenpeace
30-31 Islington Street
London N1 8XE

National Society for Clean Air
136 North Street
Brighton BN1 1RG

Tidy Britain Group
The Pier
Wigan WN3 4EX

United Kingdom Atomic Energy
  Authority
Information Services Branch
11 Charles II Street
London SW1Y 4QP

Waste Watch
26 Bedford Square
London WC1B 3HU

Friends of the Earth (Australia)
National Liaison Office
366 Smith Street
Collingwood
Victoria 3065

Greenpeace (Australia)
310 Angas Street
Adelaide 5000

Friends of the Earth (Canada)
Suite 53
54 Queen Street
Ottawa KP5CS

Greenpeace (Canada)
427 Bloor Street West
Toronto
Ontario

Friends of the Earth (New
  Zealand)
Nagal House
Courthouse Lane
PO Box 39/065
Auckland West

Greenpeace (New Zealand)
Private Bag
Wellesley Street
Auckland

Books to read

The Blue Peter Green Book by Lewis Bronze, Nick
Heathcote and Peter Brown (BBC Books, 1990)
A Cleaner World by Sarah Allen (Dinosaur/Cambridge
University Press, 1982)
The Dustbin Pack by Rob Stephenson and Harriot Blanchard
(Waste Watch, 1990)
The Green Detective in the Kitchen by Debbie Silver
(Wayland 1991)
Waste Disposal by Constance Milburn (Blackie, 1985)
The Young Green Consumer Guide by John Elkington and
Julia Hailes (Gollancz, 1990)

Picture acknowledgements
The publishers would like to thank the following for allowing their photographs to be reproduced in this book:
Bruce Coleman Ltd 9 (NASA), 22 (Norman Myers), 23 above (Norman Tomalin), 24 (Robert Carr), 34 below (Jeff
Foott), 37 below; Robert Estall *cover*; Frank Spooner Pictures 4 (Stefano Nicozzi), 15 (Eric Bouvet), 20 (Gilbert
Uzan), 32; Greenpeace 5, 19, 23 below, 31 34 above; Hutchison Library 12 (Michael MacIntyre), 23 (Lyn Gambles),
37 above; Oxford Scientific Films 7 below (Jack Dermio), 8 (Richard Kulah), 22 centre (Sean Morris), 25 above (Jack
Dermio); Photri 7 above, 14 both, 42; Rex Features 16, 17 below, 21 above and below, 33 above and below, 35, 40;
Royal Society for the Protection of Birds 43 (M W Richards); Topham Picture Library 17 above, 27, 29 below, 39, 41;
J M Wycherley 38; ZEFA 18, 36 (Deuter). The artwork is by Stephen Wheele.

Index